A Spot Under The Sun

Dr. Tanya Linzalone

978-1-961392-27-4

Dedications

This book is dedicated to my "suns", Frank and Giancarlo. You are my light and have made my days shiny and bright.

Acknowledgments

I was inspired to write this children's book for all the beautiful children with hearing loss and their resilient families that I proudly served over the years. The sun's warmth is never heard but only felt... like my love and my dedication to you and your family, To me, I only saw your light!

I am the **SUN**, a big star, so
SHINY and **BRIGHT!**
You can still feel my **WARMTH**
from far, far away!

You can't touch me and yet I see everything and everyone. From where I am, everyone looks the same.

I watch all the children play, the animals on land and in the sea. I help the grass and flowers grow. I love what I see from up here.

No one evers looks for
me but knows when I
am not around. I am
only hiding so don't be
scared when it's dark.

After the rain,
you will **FEEL**
me again.

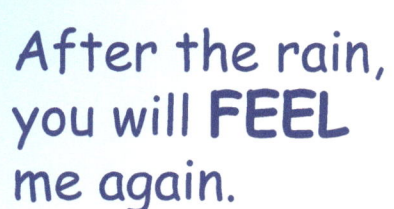

I never sleep as I travel to different places around the world at night because I brighten the sky in the morning.

Know that I will come back and the dark of night will be gone. My **LIGHT** will be waiting for you in the morning.

Even if **YOU** only feel me
know that I am near and how
important you are because...

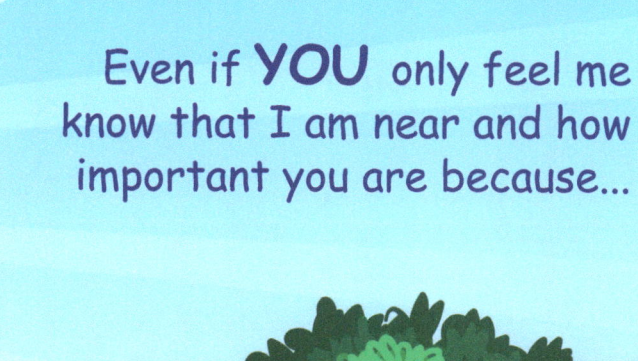

16

We are ALL children of light!

17

EVERYONE HAS A SPOT UNDER THE SUN...

...SHINE BRIGHT!

And still, after all this time,
The sun never says to the
Earth, "You owe me". Look
what happens with a love
like that, It lights the
whole sky - Hafiz.

About the Author

Dr. Tanya Linzalone has had a successful career path for the past 34 years providing hearing services to children and adults. She prides herself as a pediatric Audiologist as her love and commitment to serving children with hearing loss is evident with each child that she serves. This book was inspired by the families that she has met over the years as she has encouraged them to embrace their children and look brightly into the future. Her philosophy that every child has the birthright to succeed regardless of their diagnosis is the primary message of inclusion and diversity. She currently lives on Long Island with her two "suns", Frank and Giancarlo, a beloved mother, Carla, and her two adorable cats, Nala and Cheeto.